A Teacher Taught Them All

by Lisa Combs • illustrated by Pam Fraizer

Mr. Ronald Clark was my high school honor's English and Drama teacher, and my director in several plays. But more than that, he was a mentor to me. He help me shed my childhood fears and insecurities to step out of the shadows and into the spotlight, literally. I had become interested in drama club when my older sister had been the "prompter" for the actors in several productions. I came into high school the year after she graduated and I was determined to fill her shoes in that comfortably "behind the scenes" role. Mr. Clark asked me to read opposite those who were auditioning, and then gave me the leading role in a play for which I had not auditioned. He knew he would have to trick me into stepping outside my comfort zone. That experience changed me in ways that I could never have anticipated, giving me confidence and revealing to me that I had a voice that deserved to be heard. He passed away December 21st, 2016 and was one of the inspirations for this book.

— Lisa Combs

One of my favorite teachers was Maxine Eby, whom I had for sixth grade. She believed in me when I felt alone and out-of-place—encouraging my love of art and music. My other favorite was, her husband, Ed Eby, who was my high school choir director. They both attended my high school graduation party. As they were leaving, Mr. Eby turned and said, "Always keep a song in your heart." Hand-in-hand, they walked to their car. (They always held hands.) Both have since passed away.

*   I was fortunate enough to attend Mr. Eby's memorial service five years ago. All former choir members were asked to come forward and sing one of our Concert Choir standards, "The Battle Hymn of the Republic." I didn't want to go up, because, my voice is not like it was. But I did, and remembered every single note. I miss them, and think about them almost every day.*

— Pam Fraizer

ISBN-13: 978-1544049595

A Teacher Taught Them All

by Lisa Combs • illustrated by Pam Fraizer

"What's the most important job?"
the teacher asked my class.

And I thought about it all day long,
as the hours slowly passed.

An artist who draws or paints or sculpts?

An actor on stage or screen?

An architect planning buildings
that won't crumble, fall or lean?

A nurse who cares for the sick and lame?

A musician creating tunes?

A biologist who studies bacteria,
or an ornithologist studying loons?

Or maybe an anthropologist,
who studies other people?

Or a minister who prays with folks,
in a church with a big, tall steeple?

A conductor who leads the orchestra,
or the kind who runs the trains?

A surgeon who fixes people's hearts,
or one who fixes brains?

A engineer who builds websites,
or houses, planes, or cars?

An astronaut who goes to space,
an astronomist who studies stars?

A baker making delicious cakes?

An accountant to manage money?

A beekeeper saving the lives of bees
(who can also sell some honey)?

A beautician making people shine?
A seamstress making clothes?

A botanist who studies plants,
and creates a brand new rose?

The custodian who cleans our school,
a mechanic who fixes cars?

Or the person who takes care of all our streets,
by spreading asphalt, rock and tar?

So many careers to choose from,
and important jobs to do!
The world needs every one of them,
and values each one too.

But maybe the most important job
is one that I forgot...
...one that the others rely upon,
whether they notice it or not.

My teacher takes home bags of work,
rarely sitting at the desk.

Grading papers, planning lessons
to help each child be a success.

Making learning seem so easy,
even lessons that are tough.

Making life seem much more bearable,
on a day that might be rough.

Asking questions to make us think,
and use our imagination.

Giving us goals to guide our lives,
and the skills to lead our nation.

The world needs lots of teachers,
teaching kids of every kind.

Helping students learn and grow
in body, heart and mind.

Teachers have the biggest job,
Summer, Winter, Spring or Fall.

Without them, the rest would not exist,
because a teacher taught them all!

Lisa Combs

is an educator, advocate for children,
and owner of Combs Educational Consulting, Ltd.
To learn more about Lisa, visit her website at:
www.combseducationalconsulting.com

Pam Fraizer

is a graphic artist, illustrator,
and owner of FraizerDesigns, LLC.
To see more of Pam's art, visit her website at:
www.fraizerdesigns.org

Visit us both at www.bestfriendbooks.com

Made in the USA
Lexington, KY
08 August 2017